Cozy Cottages

Adult Coloring Book

By Beth Ingrias

Want to color more for FREE?

Get a FREE 25 page adult coloring book

visit

www.BethIngrias.com

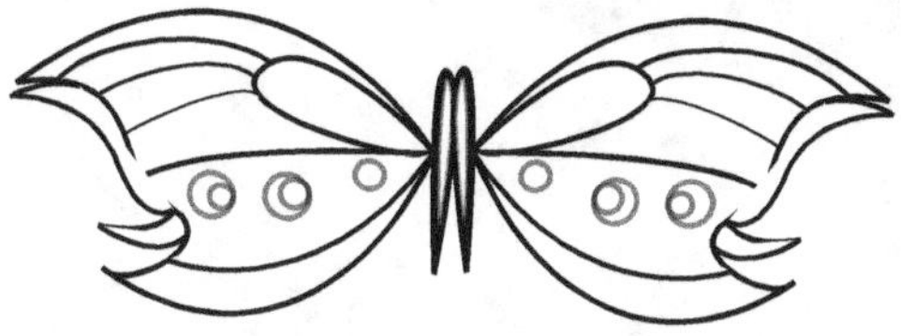

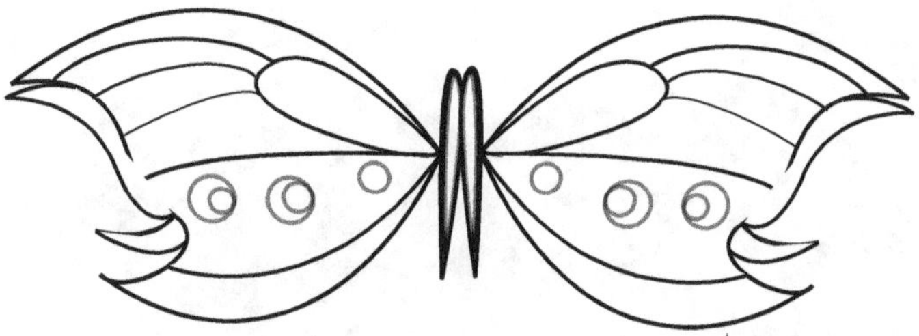

ISBN-13: 978-1-945803-47-5
ISBN-10: 1-945803-47-9

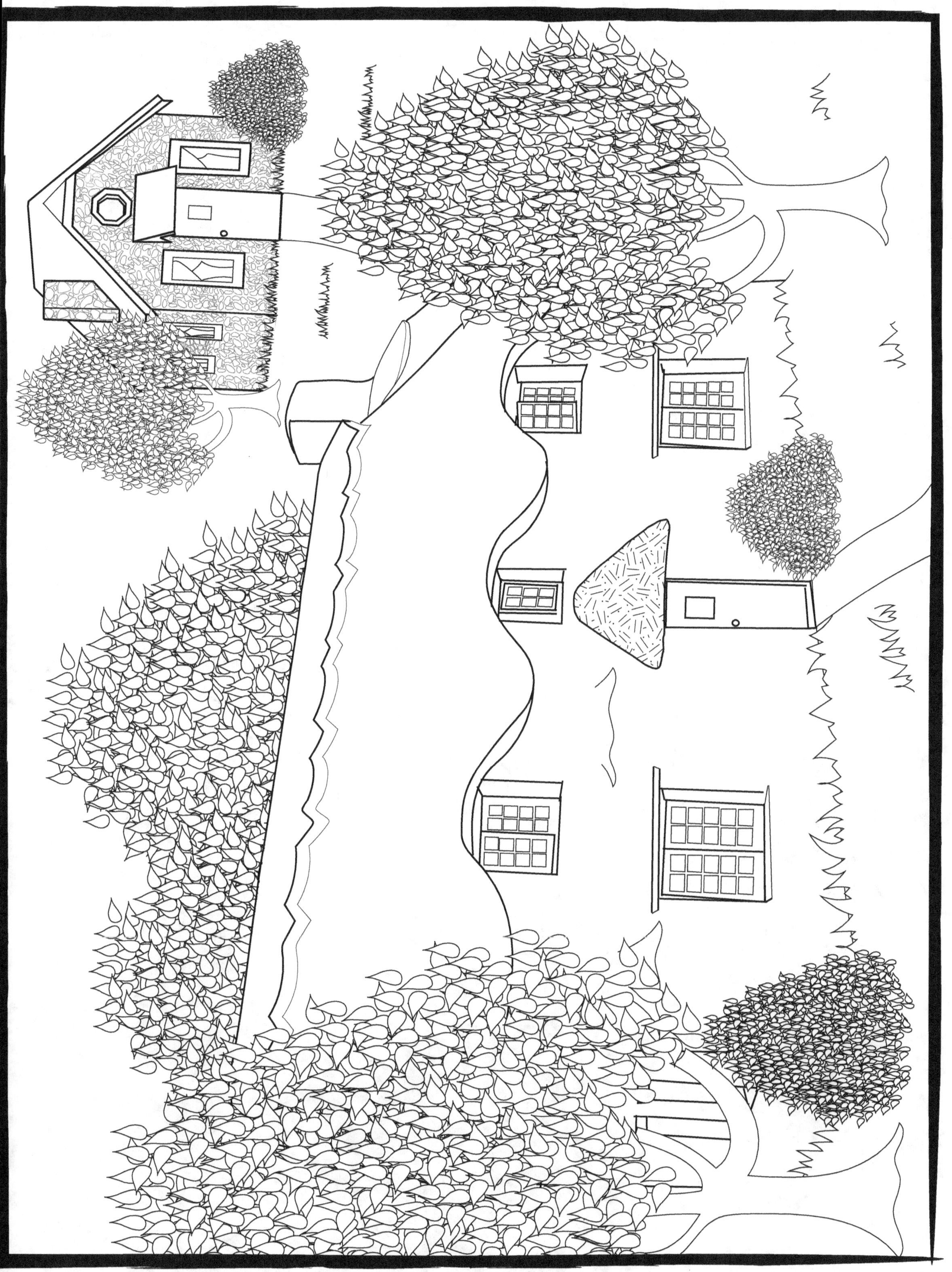

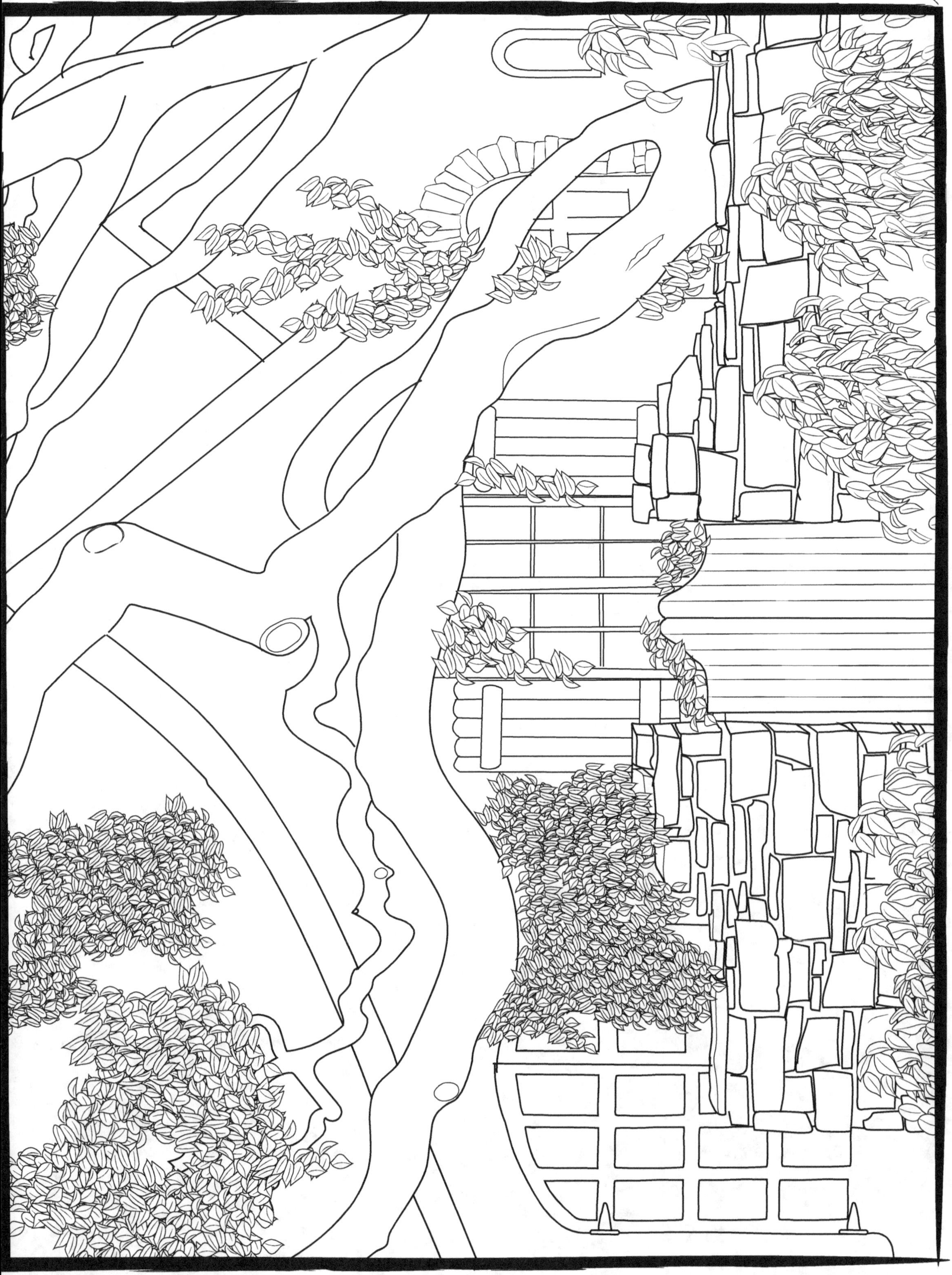

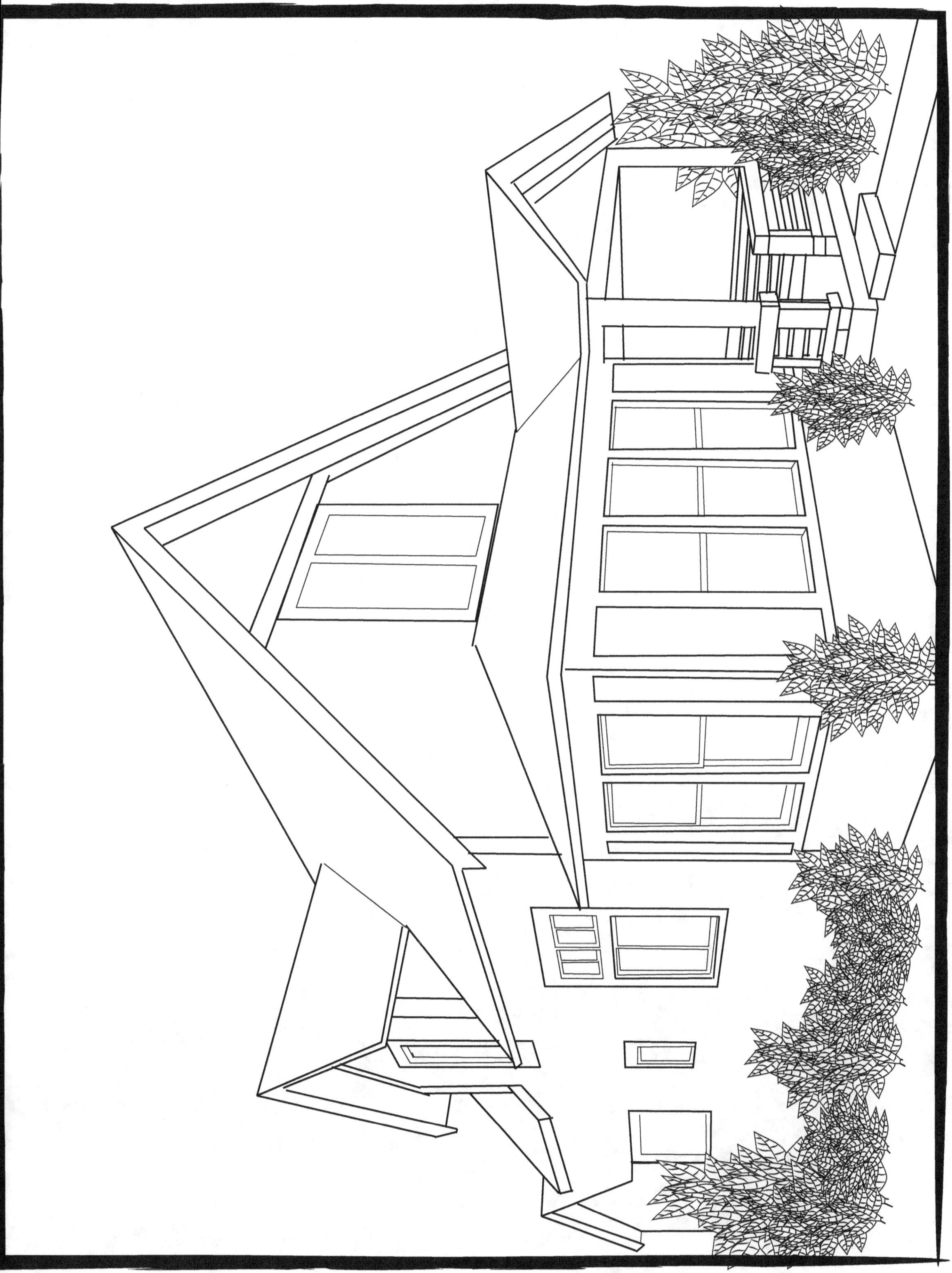

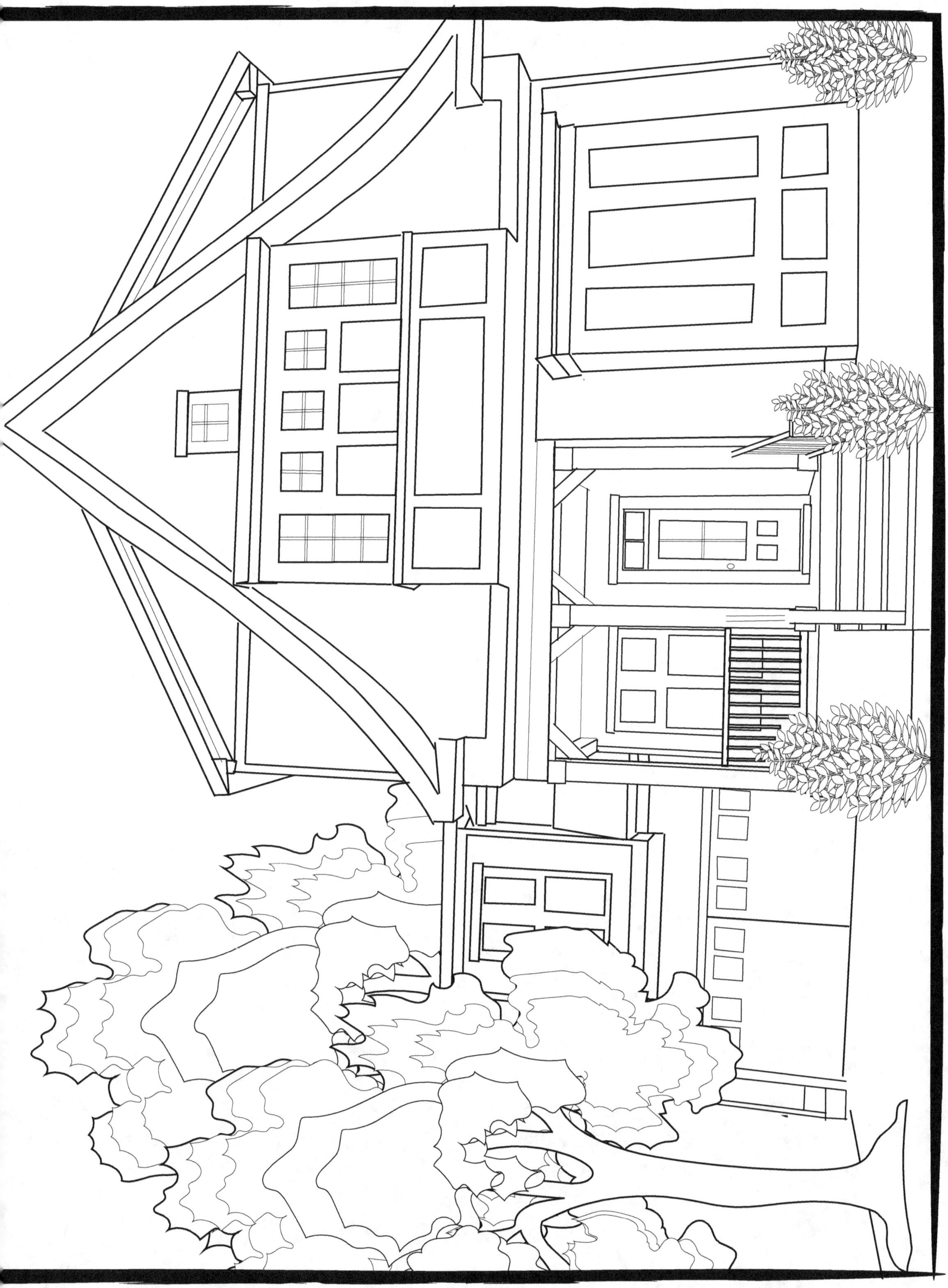

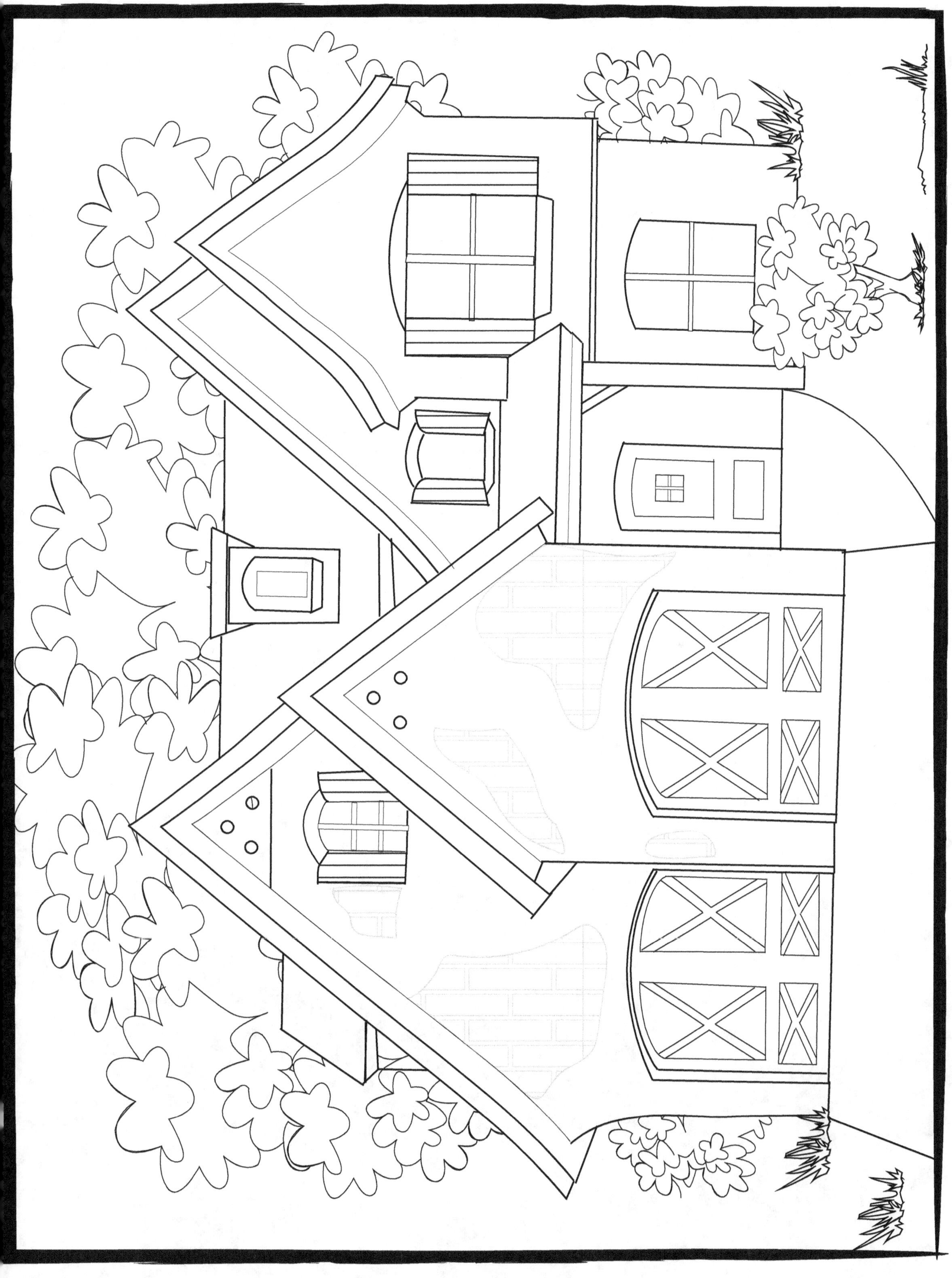

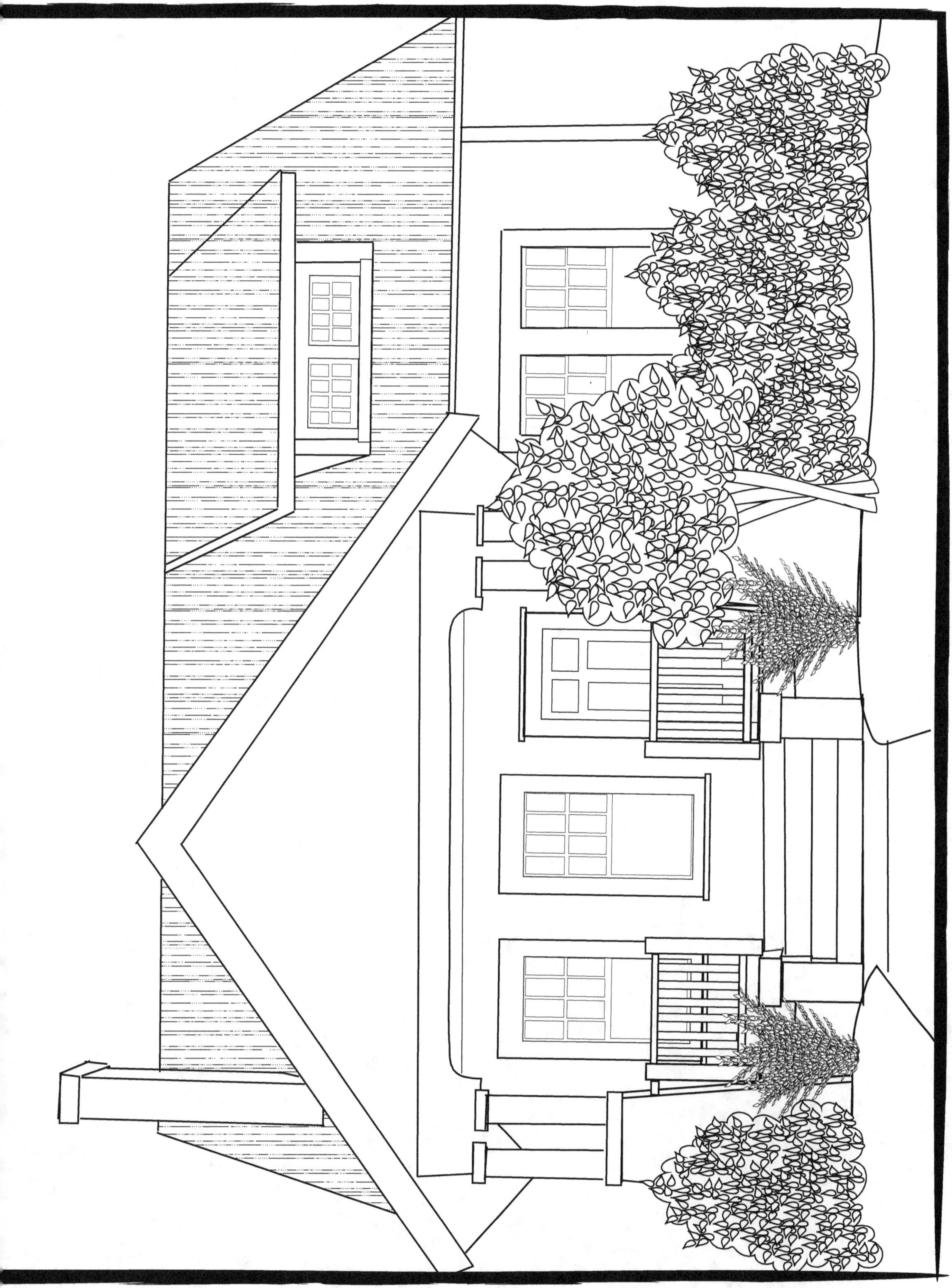

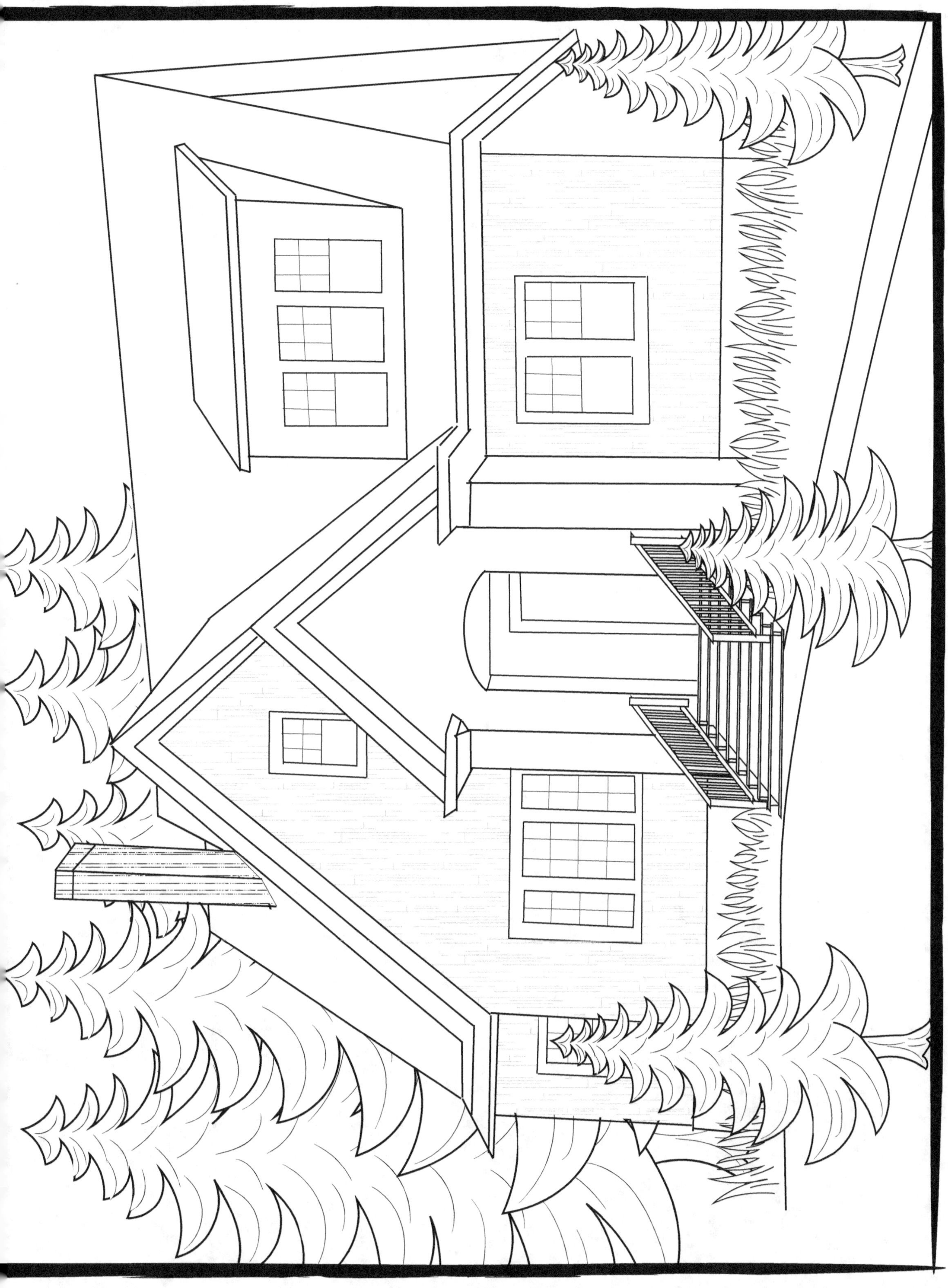

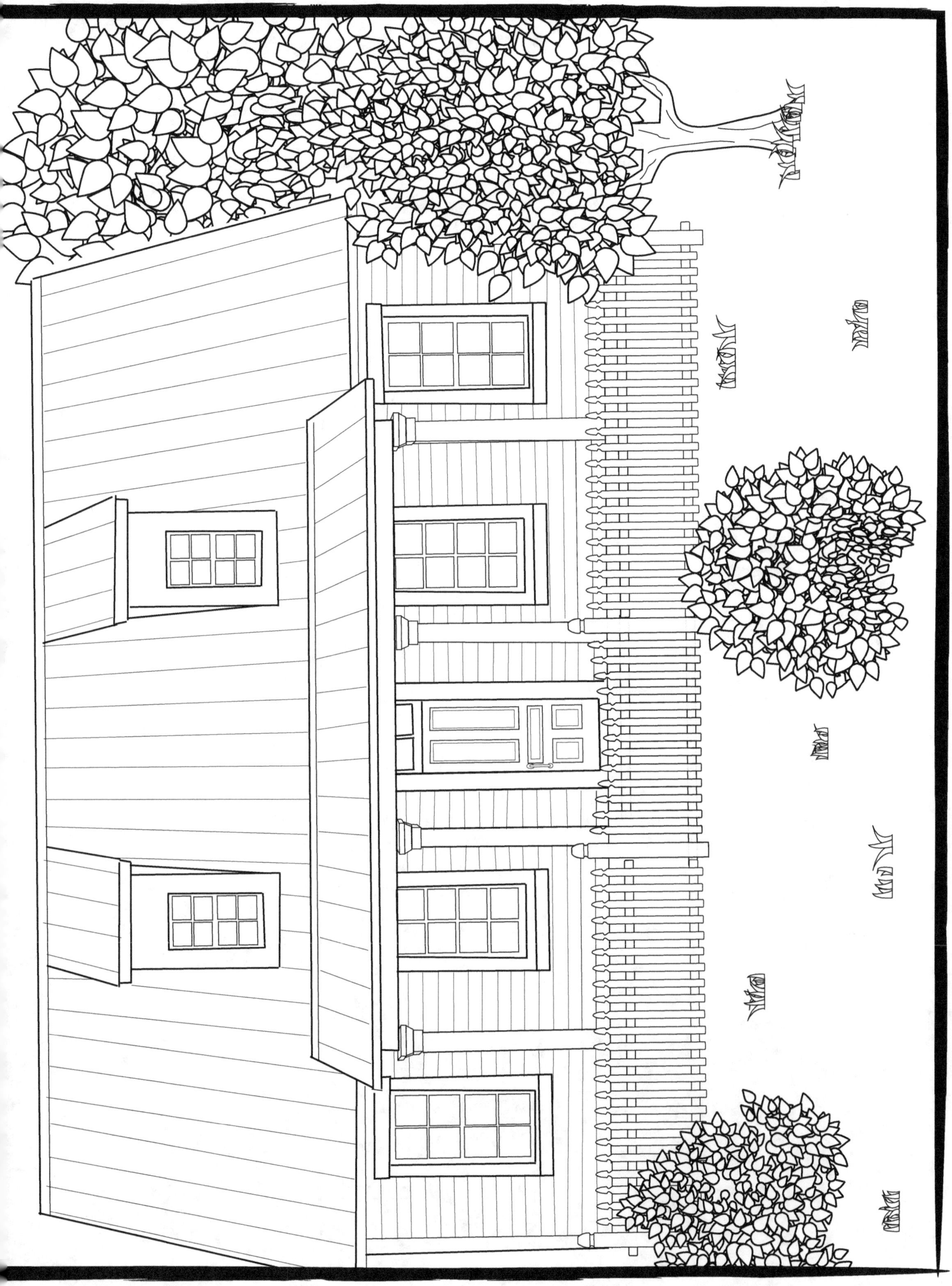

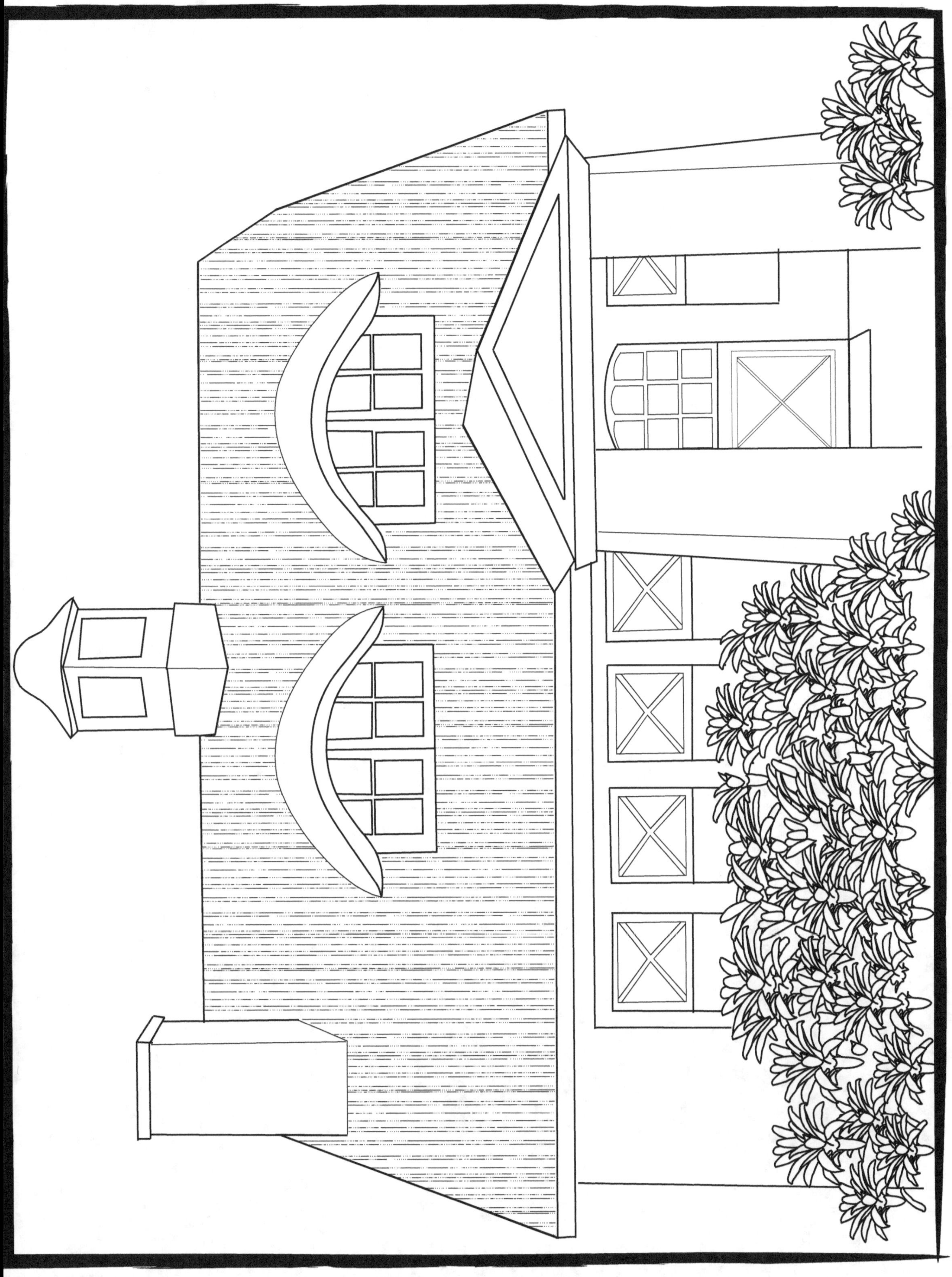

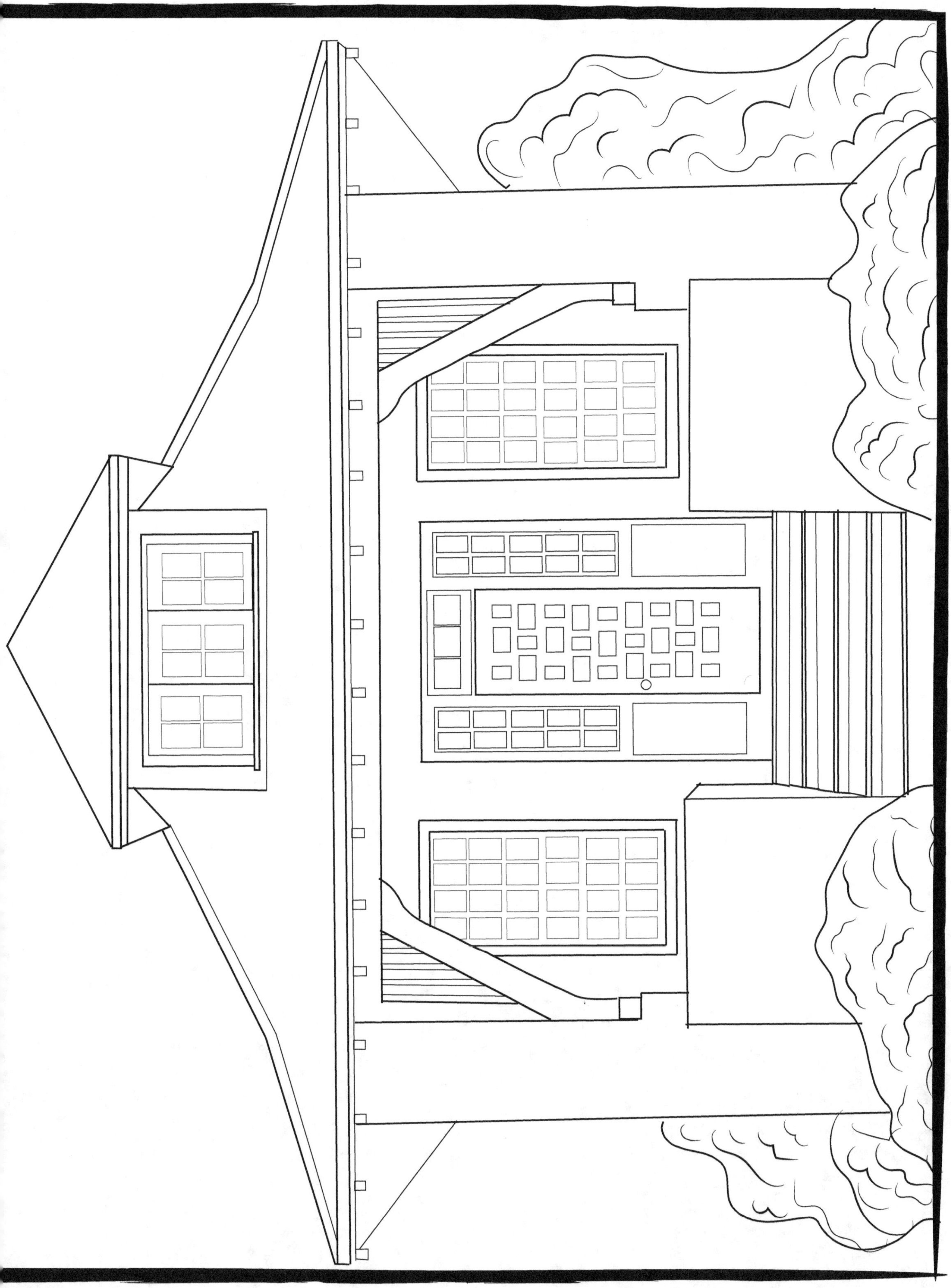

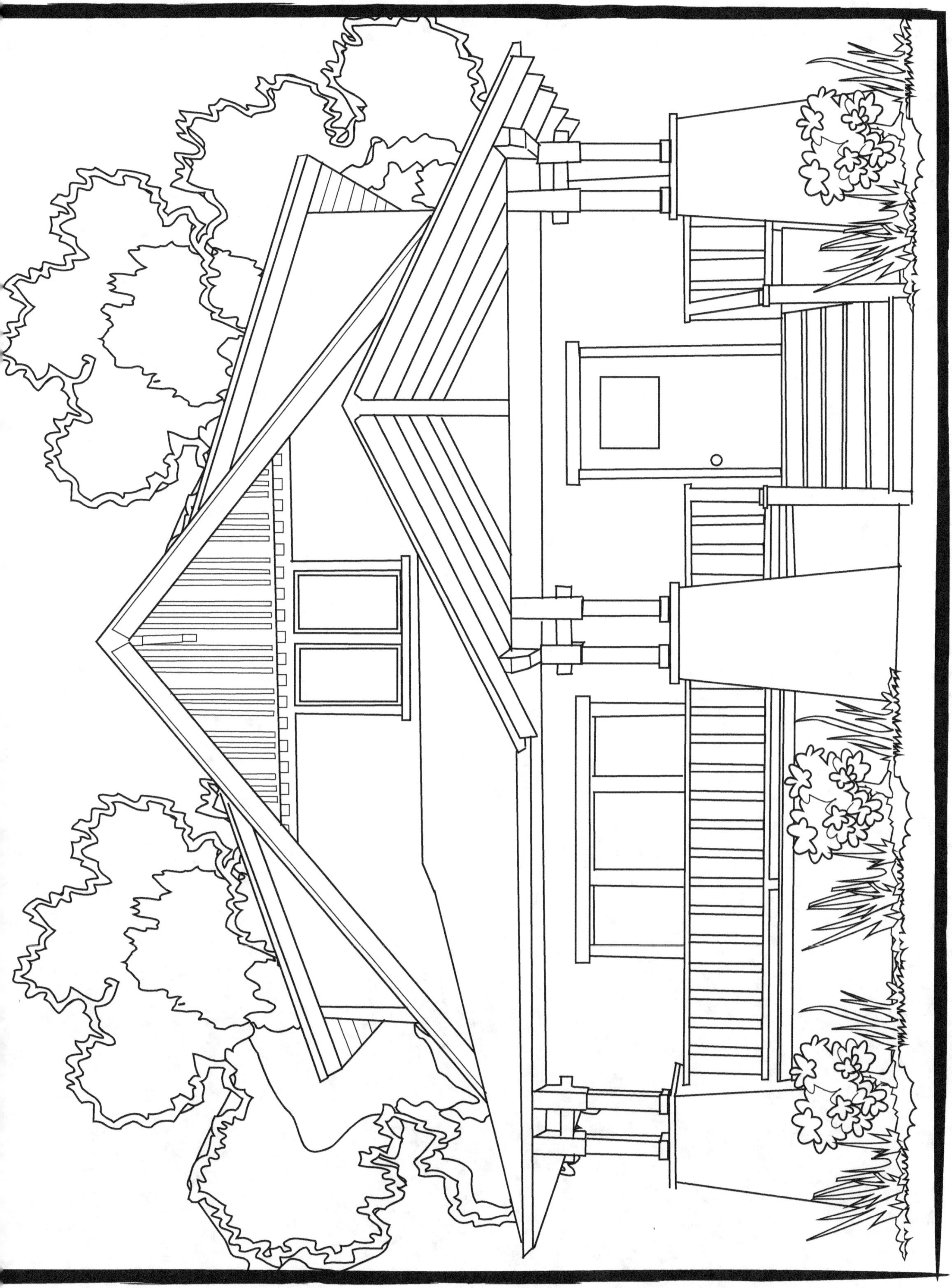

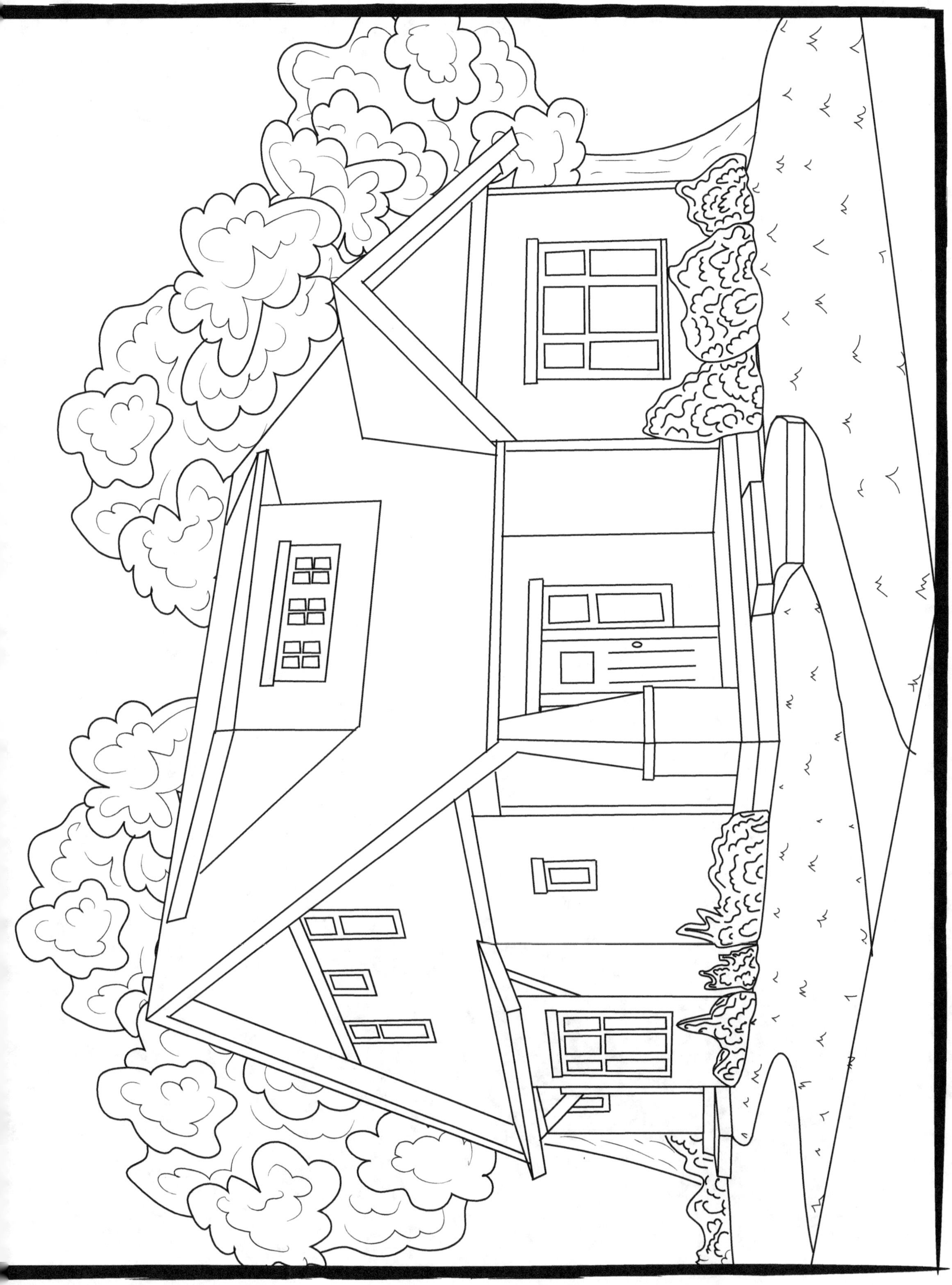

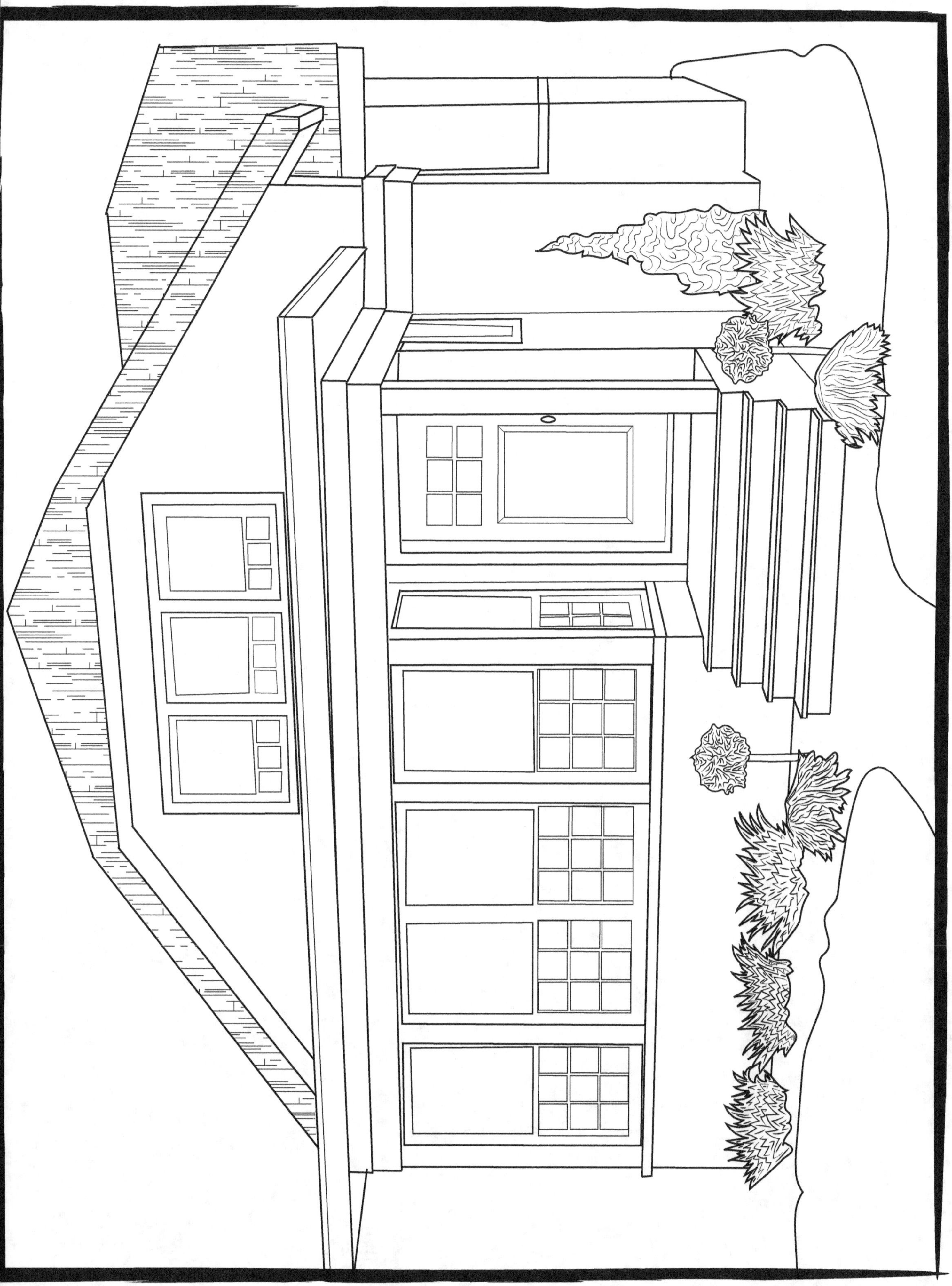

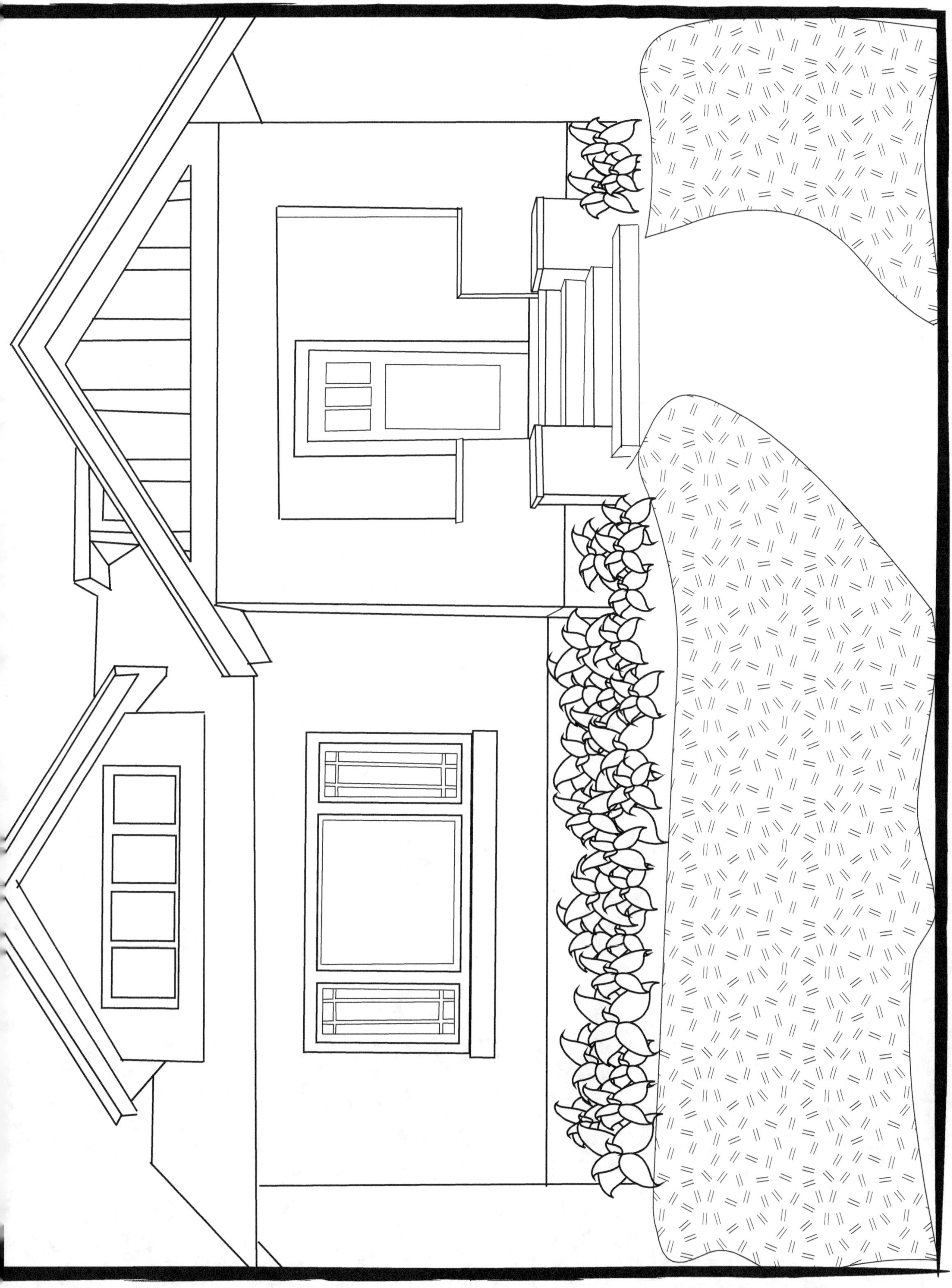

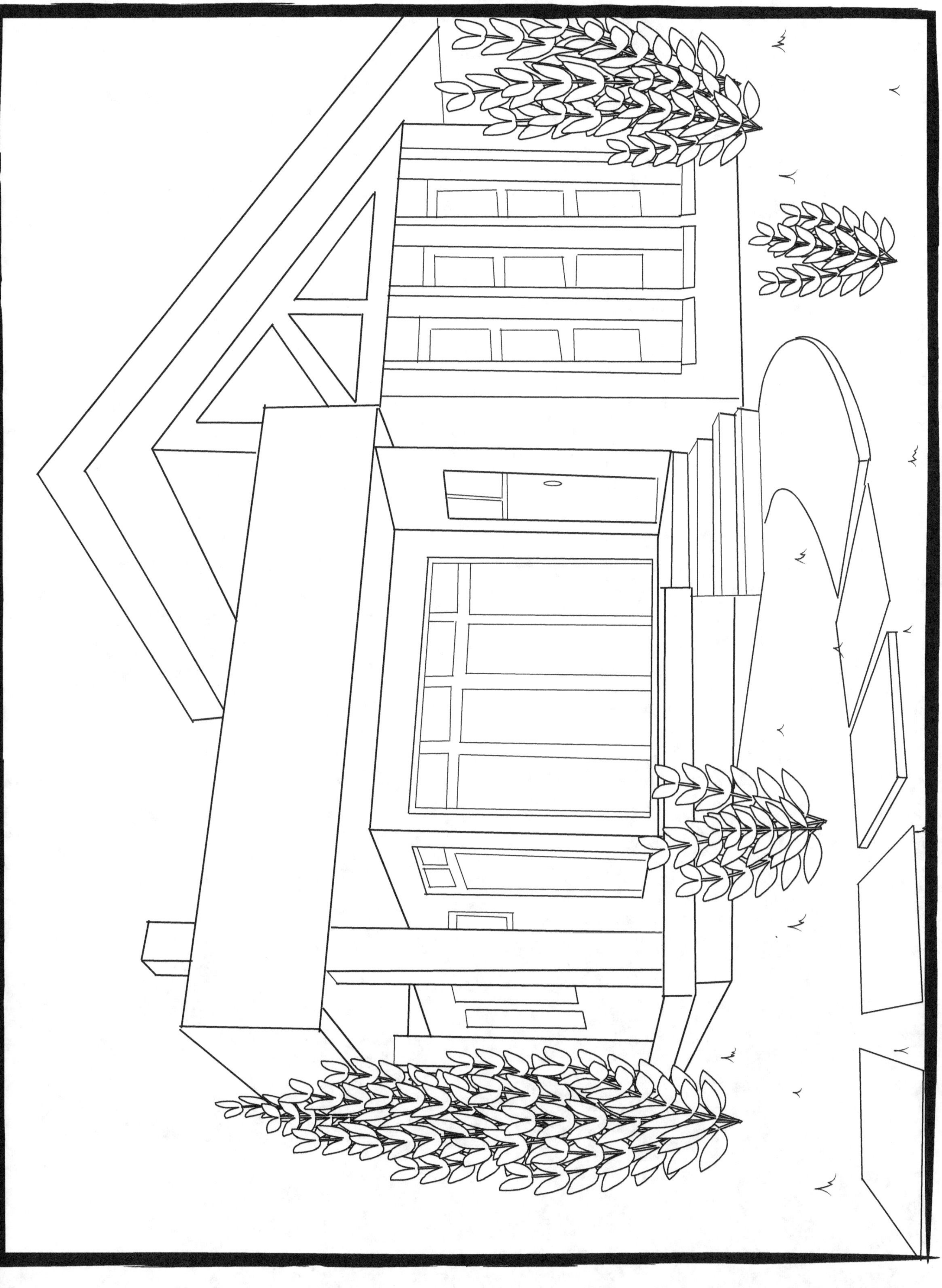

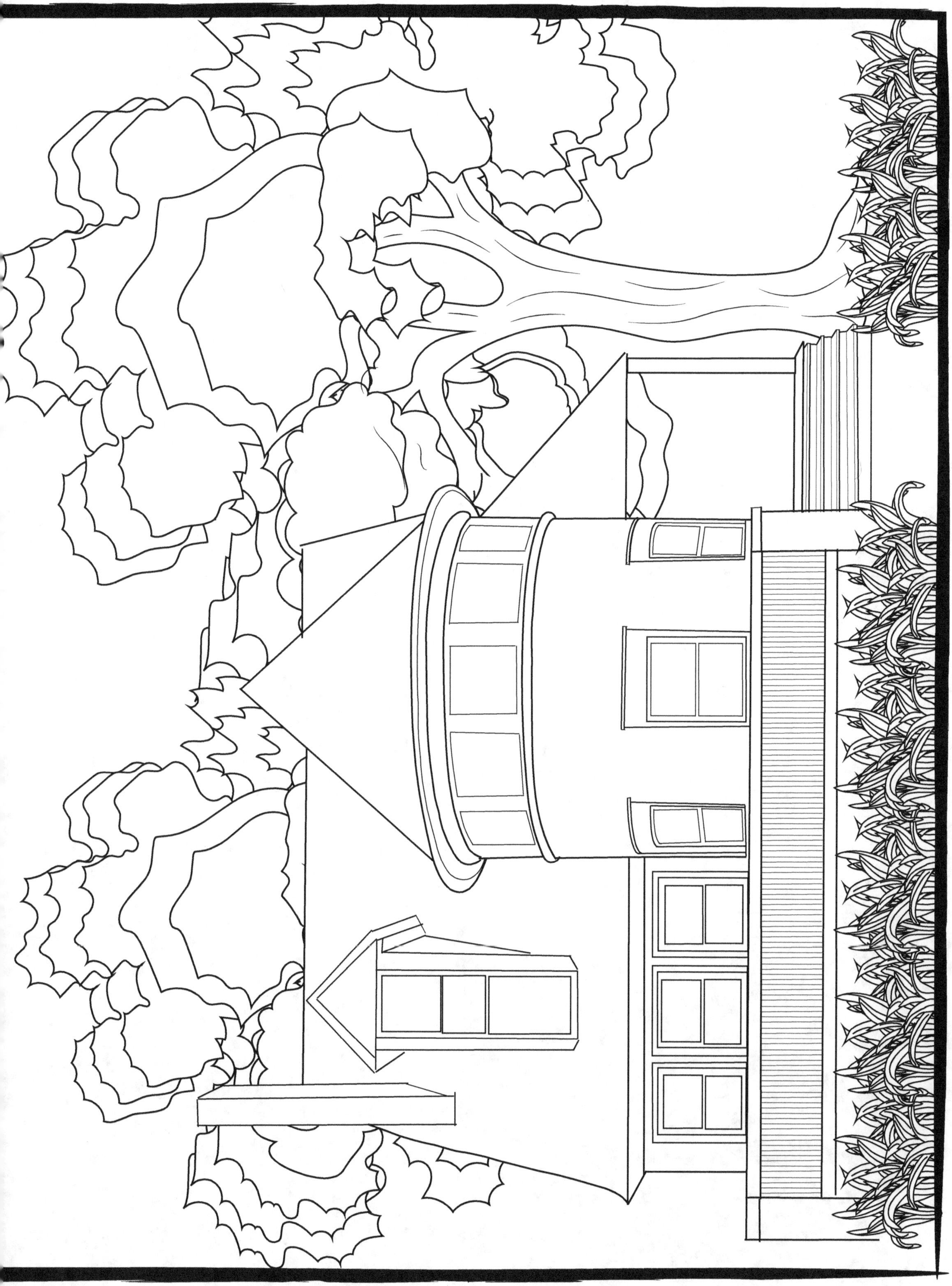

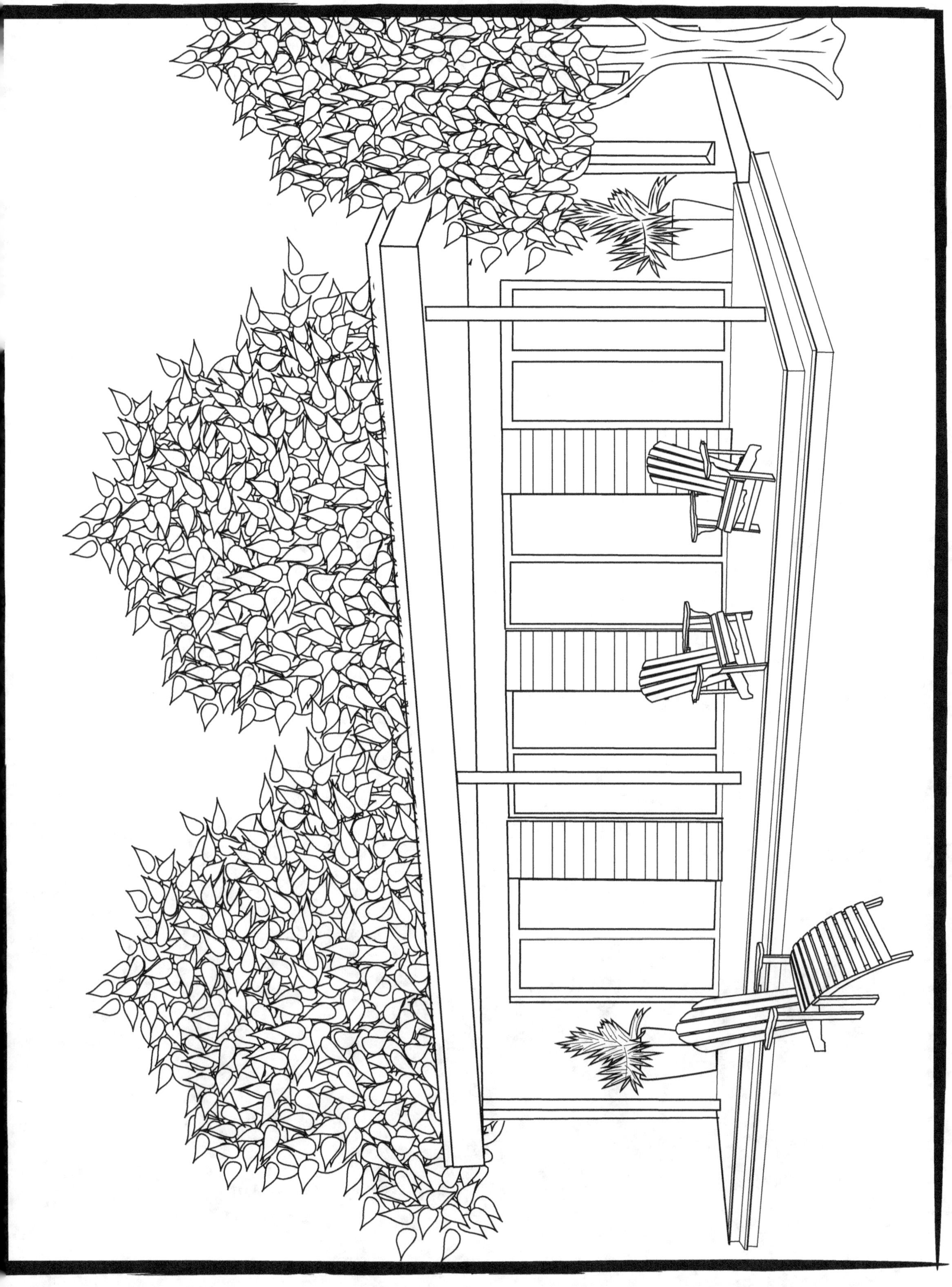

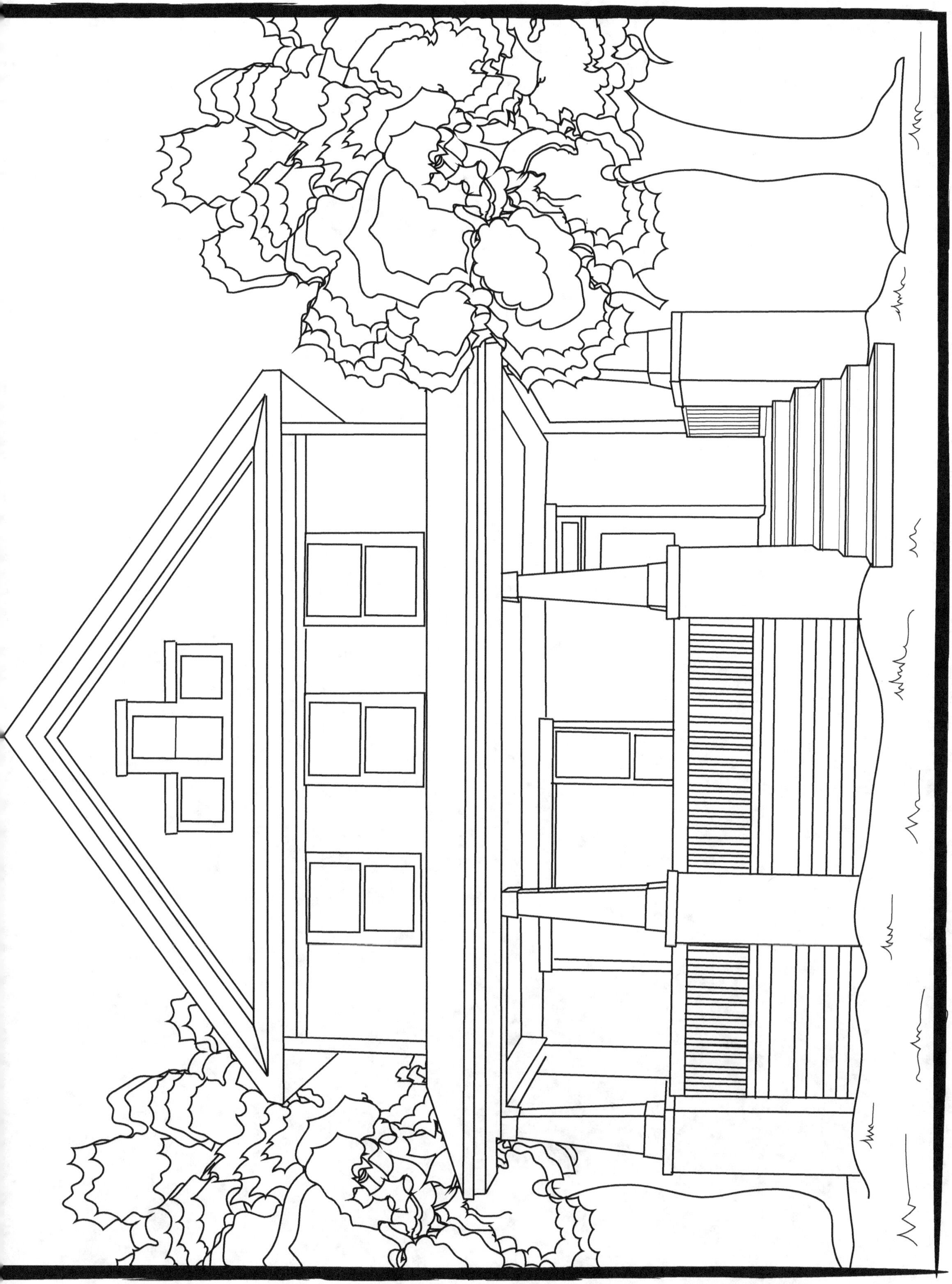

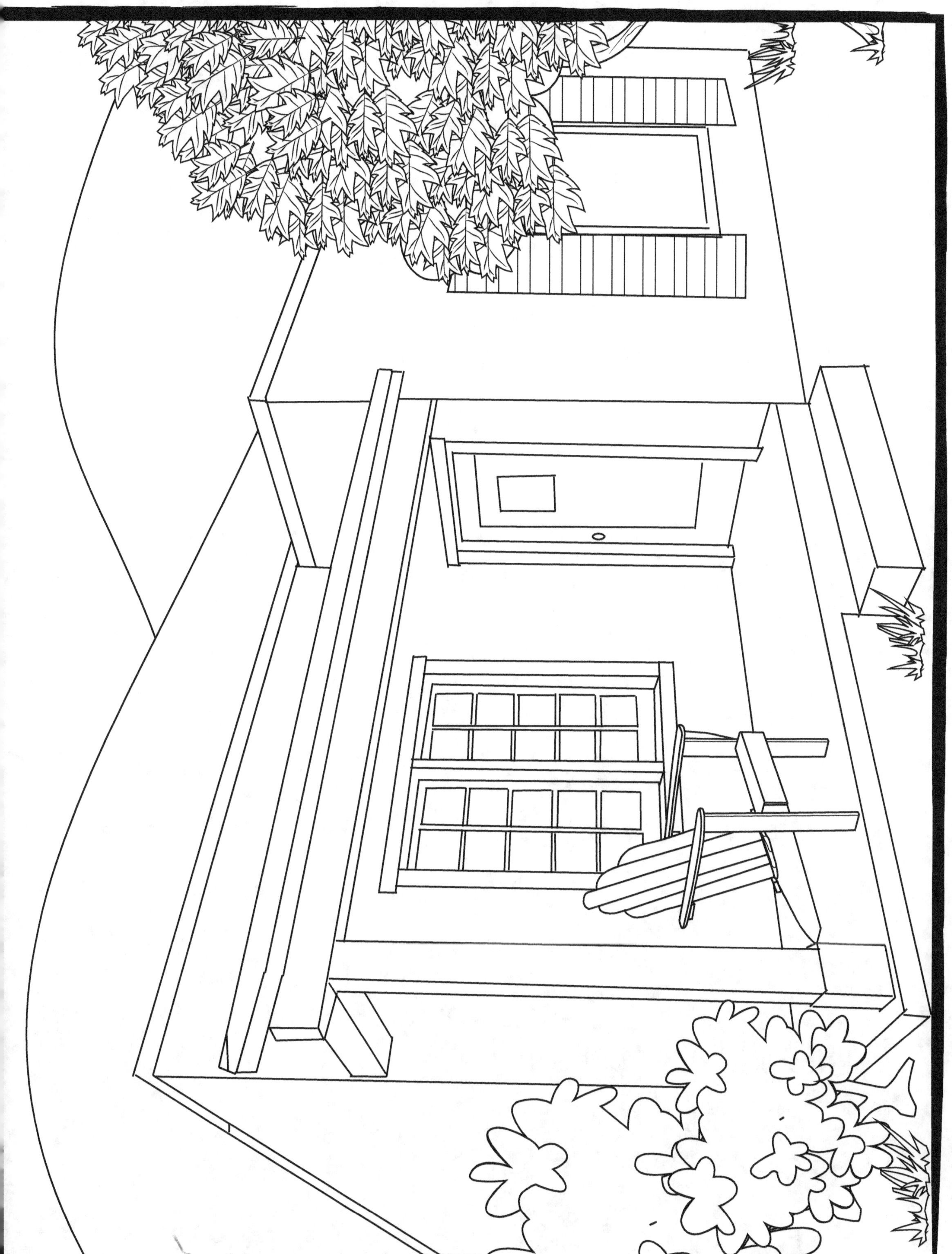

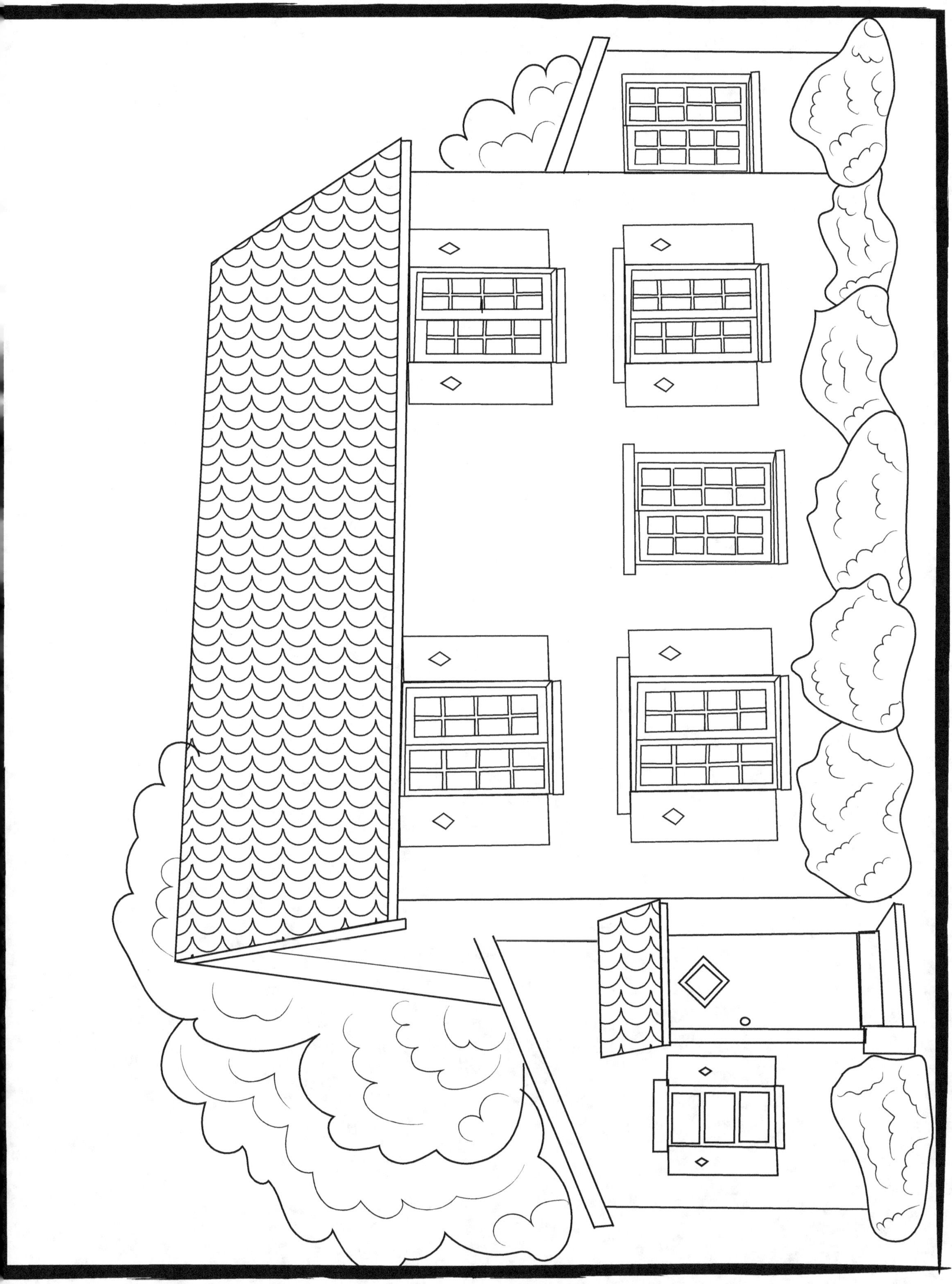

www.ingramcontent.com/pod-product-compliance
Lightning Source LLC
Chambersburg PA
CBHW081622220526
45468CB00010B/2995
* 9 7 8 1 9 4 5 8 0 3 4 7 5 *